Copyright © 2017 by Lori DiPasquale

This book may not be reproduced in whole or in part in any form or by any means, electronic or mechanical, including photocopying, recording, or by any information storage and retrieval system now known or hereafter invented, or otherwise be copied for public or private use without written permission from the publisher, except in the case of brief quotations, reviews and certain other noncommercial uses permitted by copyright law. This book is intended only as an informative guide for those looking to purchase a vehicle. The information in this book is general and is offered with no guarantees on the part of the author. The author and publisher disclaim all liability in connection with the use of this book.

Paperback ISBN : 978-0-692-87288-8

Visit us Online! www.girlsguidetocarbuying.com

Contents

Introduction	4
Buying Basics	
Budget	8
Budget Planner Worksheet	
Fuel Expense Worksheet	
Financing	13
Purchase Planner Worksheet	
Research "The One"	18
Vehicle Research Checklist	
Online Valuations	22
History Reports	26
Negotiating A Bad History Report	
It's What's On The Inside That Counts 💕	30
Trading In	33
Current Vehicle Value Worksheet	
Why Buy Used	36
Pre-Purchase Checklist	
Preparation	39
Buyer's Questionnaire	
Warranties	43
Buyers Guide Examples	
Hook Line & Sinker - Don't take the bait	48
Closing The Deal	50
Resources	

www.girlsguidetocarbuying.com

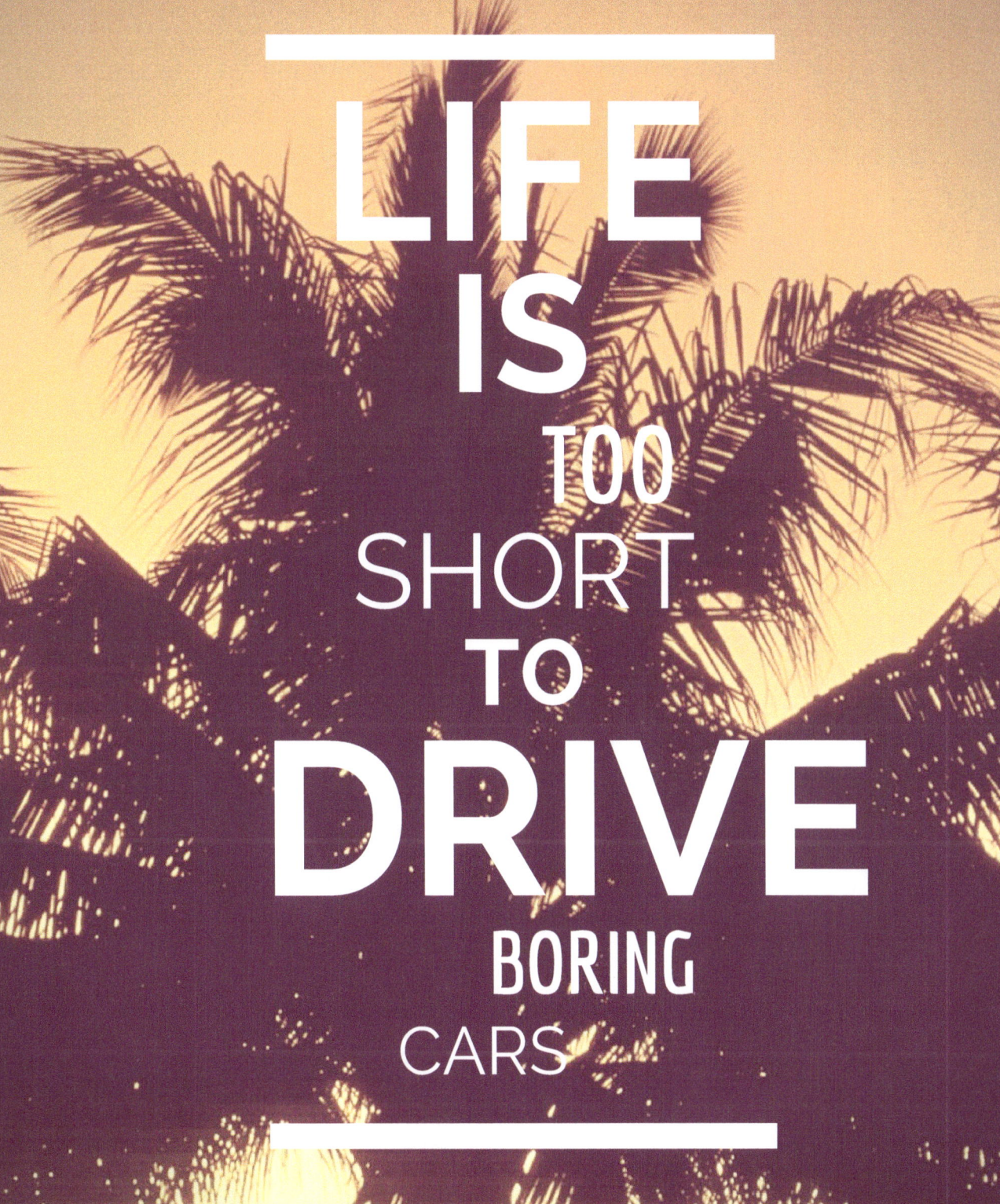

Intro

So it all started back in the awesome decade of the 1980's. I was raised in an abyss of cars, as far as my little eyes could see. It was always fun to me, like a never ending adventure. I guess you could say I was somewhat of a tomboy. As you can imagine I was driving anything with wheels by age 9. I can remember during the summer months my dad would let me drive old junks inside our junkyard and take customers around to find parts. Oh how I miss the good old days! We would surely be arrested for letting our kids do what our parents let us do back then. Looking back it was some of the most wonderful memories I can remember of my Dad and me. Maybe that is why I hold cars and everything about them so close to my heart. Fast forward 30 something years later to 2017 and here I am, my entire life in and around cars. I tried other jobs and careers but I always came back. My love of fast cars and everything in between has brought me right here, exactly where the universe wanted me to be. I finally found my own little piece of an industry mostly dominated by men and worked my ass off to get here. I am extremely proud of my accomplishments and now my business is to help all individuals have an amazing, fun and unforgettable experience when buying a vehicle. My mission is to inform you of strategic steps so you can purchase with confidence and clarity all while unlocking your inner negotiator.
Follow this interactive workbook to give you the fearlessness to get what you want!

Let's Roll….

Surround yourself with the Things you love. Discard the rest. ♥

Good Vibes Only

Your vehicle is an extension of you, your personality, and says something about you. So if you're fun and free spirited you would definitely want a vehicle that expresses that. If you are all business you will want a sleek ride that is representative of your bad ass business self. The truth is we spend a lot of time in our vehicles and for some it is the only time we get to be alone and free. There is nothing like turning the radio up, putting the windows down and screaming the lyrics to your favorite song on the open road. It is very therapeutic and can mean the difference of feeling good or staying stuck in a shitty mood. Never underestimate the power of music and wind in your hair! I have done a ton of soul searching on long rides behind the wheel of vehicles that made me feel free. This is just another reason why I think I love cars, my job and driving, so much. It is a total release of all the pressures of everyday life. What vehicle that is, is different for all of us and that is why I implore you to get behind the wheel and be fearless in the pursuit of what sets your soul on fire.

Sometimes all you need is a ride in your car to cure whatever is ailing you so pick a perfect match. This is why having a vehicle that brings you debt or gives you a sense of buyer's remorse can bring a bad vibe every time you get in or look at it. The key is to have all around goodness, and your car is no exception. When you travel with positive thoughts they will follow wherever your path may lead you. I wrote this book to help you find your way to the perfect purchase of a vehicle that inspires you to feel good about YOU and your choices.

"Enjoy The Ride." You only get one spin around so make it count!

Happy Driving

Don't Save What Is Left After Spending. Spend What Is Left After Saving.

-Warren Buffet

Budget

What is your budget? This is the most important aspect of the equation. This answer will determine what vehicle you will purchase, the mileage on that vehicle (if used) your monthly allowance and your down payment. Always have your budget in check before spending time researching and looking at vehicles. It's best to know exactly what you can afford so you can plan accordingly and not be strapped for cash. Don't waste your precious time looking at things that are totally out of your price range right now, but always be aspiring to get those things you want. If you plan your purchase budget right you can keep climbing towards your higher goals by taking on manageable pieces and not setting yourself up for setbacks and monetary losses. Be smart AND stylish without breaking the bank.

This is important: make sure to allot for sales tax, documentation and motor vehicle fees as well as any additional expenses they may charge. If you are financing, these should or could be included so you don't have to pay out of pocket, but be clear in all of the terms with the lender. Be sure to ask for ALL fees from the dealer so you know the bottom line. You don't want any surprises. Also question any charges that are optional that you do not have to purchase but are listed on the bill of sale. Don't pay for things that aren't required by law or necessary for you to feel comfortable with your purchase.

You must remember to add the expenses of your monthly gas costs, daily mileage, parking, tolls or storage of the vehicle. Do anticipate unforeseen repair costs and daily maintenance to keep your vehicle in good running condition.

> **TIP:** *What is your current vehicle's MPG vs. the vehicle you want to purchase? Will you be saving money or budgeting for a higher expense?*

Also if you are financing you will have to get full insurance coverage and you want to prepare for that monthly expense. Make sure to not get a quote but an actual amount--they can be two very different numbers! This will be another factor to maintain your budget plan.

You want to budget properly and not just go out and buy something totally unprepared and have morning-after regrets. They will have a lasting effect hurting you in the long run. Take your time and go over everything thoroughly and make sure the numbers make sense before you jump in the driver's seat and head into the sunset.

Income

- Salary
- Other

Total Income
−
Total Expenses
=
Total

Goals

Notes

Expenses

Utilities

Debts

Transportation

Housing

Personal

HOW TO CALCULATE YOUR FUEL EXPENSE

Miles Per Week _____ ÷ Miles Per Gallon (MPG) _____

X $ _____ Cost Per Gallon

= $ _____ /week

figure Yours Here
>>>>>>>>>>>>>>>>>>>>

Use an online cost of gas calculator to tell you what you will spend monthly and annually on gas.
Have the estimated average cost per gallon / The miles driven per month And miles per gallon of vehicle

---

Properly inflated tires can enhance your fuel efficiency.
Check tire pressure monthly.

A BIG PART OF FINANCIAL FREEDOM

IS HAVING YOUR HEART & MIND

FREE FROM WORRY ABOUT THE WHAT - IFS OF LIFE

—SUZE ORMAN

Financing

If you are going to finance the purchase of your new or used vehicle you need to do some homework on YOU first. Know Your Numbers! Like what is your credit score and your debt-to-income ratio. These will be major factors in determining your rate and term of your loan. The last thing you want is to go asking for money and have no idea about yourself. You should know more about your current financial situation than anyone else. Certainly don't go asking people what your self worth is, we all know how that story ends. So get Prepared!

Your credit score is a mathematical prediction of your ability to pay your debts. This helps the lender determine your spending habits, how much debt you have and how well you pay on the debt. This number will be a factor in determining your finance rate, and how long they are willing to extend the time to pay off the loan. Higher credit scores can get the creme de la creme options, but only if you know what your numbers will get you first. Your lack of knowledge in this area will get you screwed. They will be able to tell right away if you know what you're worth. Stick up for yourself and get what you qualify for or better.

The whole debt-to-income ratio is simply a measure of risk and financial stability. All you would do to figure this number is add up all your recurring debt like mortgage, rent, credit cards etc., and divide it by your gross monthly income.

$$DTI = \text{Total Monthly Debt Payments} / \text{Gross Monthly Income}$$

The lower the DTI the less risk you are to a lender. When your DTI is higher than the suggested percentage, reach out to credit unions and smaller banks to see if they will work with you. Typically they have more leniency to accommodate a higher DTI percentage.

TIP: *Use a debt-to-income ratio calculator to compute your DTI for you.*

There are two ways you can obtain financing for your vehicle. The first way is through the dealer and is called *Indirect lending.* This is typically the most common way consumers get financed for auto purchases. I believe not because they have the best deal but purely out of convenience and unpreparedness of the consumer. Here It all happens under the same roof as the dealership and everything is handled in house. The dealer collects your information, puts it into a lending pool and shops the loan. The lenders will reply with a "buy rate" which is a **minimum** interest rate that the dealer can then add to and is typically compensated for facilitating the indirect financing method.

Direct lending is when consumers will go in search of their own lending and find the best deal through credit unions, banks, and online institutions.

I highly encourage obtaining financing this way. Have your financing in place before you do any shopping. Visit your local credit union or bank of choice and find the best rate so you know ahead of time what to expect. You NEVER have to finance with a dealership. It is just an option they provide and it is usually a higher rate with added fees. However if you shopped your loan you already have your rate locked in. Use it as a negotiating tool to see if the dealer can get you an even lower rate. Just beware of fine print and fees, make sure to read over everything and ask questions.

Now, your monthly payments will be determined by the amount put down, how long the loan will be and the rate of the loan. Typically the longer the length of the loan the lower the monthly payments but the more paid overall. Higher payments and a shorter term will get the vehicle paid off faster, paying less interest over the length of the loan. Usually this will result in the vehicle having equity, giving you an option to sell or trade it for cash value towards your next purchase.

I always suggest putting down a substantial comfortable amount to get some equity into it straight away. The worst outcome is the vehicle being worth less than you owe or the loan outliving the life of the vehicle. Both of these are a less than desirable outcome and could cause havoc on your budget.

Be wary of gap insurance, extended warranties, and vehicle add ons. These are where the money is made. Do your due diligence and say NO to what you do not want or need. Check out my resources page for some independent companies that supply warranties, insurance and all kinds of nifty things to protect your vehicle all at comparable prices. Some are even easy to use apps.

It's always wise to take time to think about additional options and not make any rash decision under pressure. They are always things that can be added later down the road.
With all that in place you know exactly what you're getting into and how much you can afford so you don't break the budget and find yourself strapped every month.

I always suggest getting a better deal if you're paying cash! It won't always happen but you should try and maybe they can incorporate some of the extra costs into the final lower cash price.

If you're willing to walk away, as I think you should be, you're more likely to get the deal you want. Either by losing that one to find a better one or by getting what you asked for.

Purchase Planner

Some may not apply

Credit Score _____   Approved Finance Amt. _____   Rate _____

Price of Vehicle _____

Value Of Trade _____

Admin. Fee _____
(Taxed in State of NJ)

Balance _____ X _____
(State Sales Tax Rate ex: 6.875%)

Sales Tax _____

Balance + Sales Tax = $ _____

Motor Vehicle Fee _____

Balance _____

Cash Down _____

Total Balance Due $ _____

Total Financed Amount _____ Term _____ Monthly Payment _____

Final Rate (APR) ____ Finance Charge _____ Total Payment of Loan _____

Added Costs

Insurance _____ (full coverage if financing)

Factory Warranty _____ Dealer Warranty _____ Non-Dealer Warranty _____

Maintenance/ Repairs _____   Inspection Fee _____

Gas Expense _____   Parking/Storage/Tolls _____

Notes: _____
_____
_____

* Check with your state's Dept. of Motor Vehicle for what fees can be taxed and the sales tax rate for your state

Your Knowledge **is one** *of your most* valuable *assets*

Research "The One"

Now, some of you know how you get when you or someone close to you starts dating someone new and you turn into a straight up FBI agent, finding out all kinds of personal information and digging up all the dirt. Well it's the same for your ride, you have to get that momentum going and do the work to find out all the specifics. Pick your car like you would pick your partner. Know what you want out of your vehicle in all areas then narrow it down to a couple or one particular make and model. Get in the vehicle and really examine everything, take your time and even notes. I can't tell you how many cars I get in and the pedals are so high and far apart that I have to elevate my foot the entire time I'm driving (so uncomfortable to me). Or I absolutely hate how the controls work or where they are located, or even worse the cupholder situation (oh yes, that will kill the love right there!) Make sure to find out about all the little things like gas mileage, safety rating, resale values and all around feedback on the vehicle. A small unacceptable feature can ruin your exciting dream car purchase plan. Don't waste your time and effort researching any deeper into a vehicle without doing the leg work first.

Go schedule a test ride online at a dealership near you and do not feel the need to get into any particulars with the salesman/woman. Keep it short and sweet…you are test driving a bunch of different models and not looking to buy for several more months, PERIOD. Control the situation! Don't be rude but be firm and confident.

Once you have picked "the one" start looking for that car online and list all the prices, mileage and options, etc., into your **Vehicle Research Checklist**. If you find one that is noticeably less, make sure to check that it has a clean history report. Some will have it listed right on the advertisement but others you may have to call and ask some questions. I suggest only purchasing history reports and doing extensive checks on the actual vehicles you are considering for purchase.

You want them all to be as similar as possible, sometimes even the color will make a difference in the cost with certain makes and models! Compare apples to apples in this process so you can be as accurate as possible when it comes to negotiating time.

The time of year, where you live, and current market will play a role in the pricing of vehicles as well. For example a convertible for sale in December in New Jersey will do much less than one in December in Southern California. When pricing out a vehicle make sure you plan to purchase within a certain time frame. This will ensure the most accuracy and that all your hard work doesn't go to waste.

> **TIP:** *Take the asking price into consideration when deciding on a vehicle that is in high demand: it will sometimes bring more than what it is actually worth. So if this is the vehicle you're after then expect to pay up. There is nothing wrong with that--you should have what you want and what makes you happy, just don't expect a deal.*

VEHICLE RESEARCH CHECKLIST

YEAR_____**MAKE**_____**MODEL**_____

NADAguides.com VALUE_____

Vehicle 1

Mileage_____
Color_____
Options_____
Location _____
Private Seller _____
Dealer _____
Price$_____
History Report _____
Date_____
Notes:_____

Vehicle 2

Mileage_____
Color_____
Options_____
Location _____
Private Seller _____
Dealer _____
Price$_____
History Report _____
Date_____
Notes:_____

Vehicle 3

Mileage_____
Color_____
Options_____
Location _____
Private Seller _____
Dealer _____
Price$_____
History Report _____
Date_____
Notes:_____

Vehicle 4

Mileage_____
Color_____
Options_____
Location _____
Private Seller _____
Dealer _____
Price$_____
History Report _____
Date_____
Notes:_____

SOMETIMES
VALUE
ISN'T
ALWAYS
PRICE

—RENNE COON

Online Valuations

If I hear one more time, well Kelley Blue Book says…..I will literally pull some of my hair out and go into fetal position. Everyone, even lawyers, will say this valuation IS, what it's worth. Holy heck, NO!

Let's take a step back and analyze this for a minute. When you go to a general practitioner for a checkup and they say you have a serious condition, there is nothing you can do about it, do you say ok and go home without going to a professional who specializes in that field? Or perhaps get legal advice about your divorce from a trademark and patent attorney?
Yeah, no freaking way! So why would you think because you punched a few pieces of information into an automated appraisal tool that is, by the way, made to give your information to a dealer who wants to purchase it, that you will get the absolute most accurate price on the planet?

Exactly.

Listen, you can use it as a general guide but not a final accurate value by any means. You are leaving yourself wide open by letting one or a few online calculations determine the value you should be paying or selling your vehicle for. These companies are big business and they are in it to make money off of you and so are the third parties on the other end. These are not other consumers posting price points, but companies who have stakes in buying your vehicle or selling you one. Usually buying low and selling high.

All the big fancy dealerships you see on T.V. and all over the internet don't pay for them with their own money -- you helped build those by using unfair value systems they created. Yeah, feel stupid yet?
They are leaving a trail of breadcrumbs straight to their door and you are eating every piece, totally content and giving them a big old thank you.

Wake Up!

Now get online and visit big, small and medium sized companies and private sellers who are advertising the particular vehicle you want to purchase.
Fill out your **Vehicle Research Checklist** thoroughly and as accurately as possible.

If you did this correctly they should be somewhat in the same ball field, not drastically different in comparison. This will give you an estimated number to negotiate so you know where to start pricing.

> **TIP:** *Be sure to take note of the tire size, special options, engine size or anything that would make it more or less valuable. These factors could skew your price points.*

For new vehicles, for which you know the NADA value, just make sure to account for any options and add ons to be completely accurate. The devil is in the details. Look for all the hidden elements. Be sure of what you want and don't want to get the bottom line number and same with all of your comps.

> **TIP:** *Search "best new car incentives and rebates" to get a list of the current deals and offers in your zip code.*
> *They will also give you an idea of the APR% rates to compare with your financing worksheet*

Then you want to look at sites like eBay motors to see if any have actually sold and what that amount was as well as the asking price to see if those numbers jive with the comps from other sites and sellers.

The lesson in this is to mess around with the valuation tools and work them backwards and forwards to see if you have room to negotiate and how much. Remember everyone is in business to make money so they are entitled to a profit--you wouldn't work for free either. Have a realistic goal by doing extensive homework on the vehicle and knowing the price points.

Another place to look is on Craigslist. A lot of dealers will post vehicles for sale here, as well as private sellers and you may catch a really good deal. Just never agree to go see a vehicle alone or at a private residence. Always bring a wingwoman and meet at a busy shopping plaza.

This is where buying a car from a wholesaler or well established and trusted local dealer really pays big! They usually have a very low overhead and a very small staff and the savings get passed on to the consumer. That is how you get such great deals. It's the least stressful way to buy and sell your vehicles. Plus I am a huge advocate for supporting small and local businesses and putting your money back into your community and not putting those dollars into the hands of big business and corporate America. Shop Local! Check out Small Business Saturday held on the Saturday after the US Thanksgiving holiday. They usually will have awesome deals and it is a great way to help support the small and local business community!

> THE MORE YOU KNOW
> ABOUT THE PAST,
> THE BETTER PREPARED YOU
> ARE FOR THE
> FUTURE.
>
> - Theodore Roosevelt

History Report

This report tells you many things, however it's not the end all be all! A lot of things never get disclosed and therefore will never make it on the report.
  Example: You get into an accident with either a tree, deer, pole …..(you see where I'm going with this) or a fender bender with another person and you both agree to handle it between one another without reporting it. There are many reasons a person will not report accidents or call the police. It will spare them from insurance rates spiking, points on a driving record and traffic tickets, but most of all it won't devalue the vehicle with a bad history report. So there are a lot of unregistered accidents out there which means a vehicle history report isn't always a 100% guarantee that everything is good.

You always want to thoroughly go over your vehicle and check for any possible previous damage.

How to Read the Vehicle History Report

Pay attention to the dates and how close together they are for d.m.v. actions. If the title has been flipped at a motor vehicle agency consecutively several times in a row during a short period, this could mean something's up. Check where the vehicle was located before all the action started. This could indicate it was a flood vehicle and they are getting it out of the zone and back into the market.

Take advantage of checking out when the dealer purchased the vehicle for the lot, if more than three months have passed you have negotiating power. It's aged inventory and they are most likely looking to cut it loose.

Make sure to ask to see the maintenance and repair records to check if they correspond to the history report. Ask to see the window sticker/ buyer's guide and the owner's manual. These items will help verify the condition of the vehicle as well as make its resale value greater, especially exotic and high end luxury vehicles.

You also want to confirm that all recalls have been taken care of if there are any. It is not the dealer's or seller's responsibility, so be sure to check the vin# of the vehicle for recalls at safecar.gov. Do this even if you are buying a certified pre-owned (CPO) vehicle.

Negotiating A Bad History Report

If the report has damage/accident reported you have leverage for negotiating. This is only if you feel comfortable with the damage stated in the report and you feel it does not affect the safety of the vehicle. Statistics show that half of consumers would not buy a car that had been in an accident and the majority would expect a large discount to purchase one. So if negotiating is your thing, have at it!

I suggest using comps that you have found of the vehicle with clean history reports vs. bad history reports and calculate the difference in prices. Then you have a number you can negotiate on and feel comfortable you got a good deal and did not pay over what it was worth with the bad report.

Another type of listing to be wary of, or smell the potential for a deal are VHR's with rental or fleet history. Rentals and or taxi's are usually never cared for like a personal vehicle would be. The same goes for fleet, even though they are most likely a company car given to an employee who has earned this perk, it is still not their own vehicle that they had to pay for or maintain with their hard earned cash. There is something to be said for people who work hard and appreciate the value of what that money can buy them. Like I always say, you have to have some skin in the game or else it is something you can discard, lose or misuse.

Always have an independent certified mechanic you know and trust do an inspection on a vehicle you are considering before purchase. You never want to jeopardize your safety for savings!

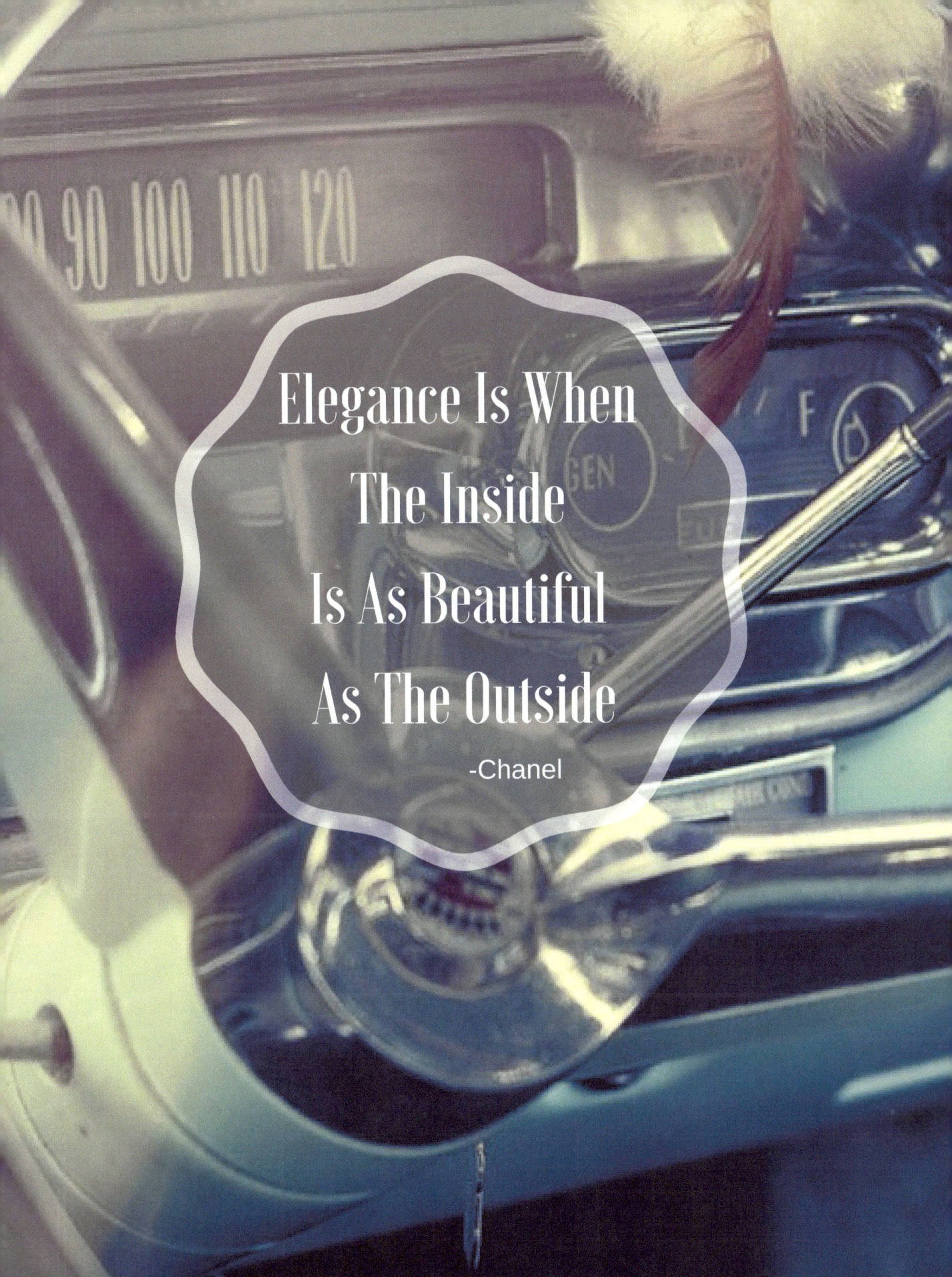

It's What's On The Inside That Counts

Just because it's pretty on the outside doesn't mean it is on the inside! Get to know your way around a vehicle. You don't have to get crazy but just get familiar with where things are and the terms associated with them. Be able to identify the important items, how they work and their purpose. This is important because a lot--I mean a ton--of vehicles look so amazing on the outside and inside (the major components) are a total mess. This stands true for the opposite as well, many vehicles look dingy on the outside and they are unforeseeably perfect inside and just in need of some tlc and a paint job.

First, pop the hood and check all the fluids, this will be a tell if the vehicle has been maintained or serviced. It may sound daunting but it is quite easy. Practice on your current vehicle or ask someone to give you a crash course. You can also study and refer to a diagram or video of that particular make and model vehicle and take notes to verify the components and fluids. It is important to know a few of these simple techniques because you never know when this knowledge may be necessary and useful for you in the future.

TIP: *Check out the upper inside left hand corner to see if there is an oil change sticker and the mileage of when it should go or should have gone in, then check the vehicle's current mileage. Is it overdue?*

Start it up and check under the hood while it's running. Listen and look for imperfections, loud defects, smoking or any noticeable flaws. Take a thorough video of the engine while it's running as well as the entire vehicle, making sure to get the body, tires and undercarriage as best as possible. This is a great way to show someone later who may have extensive knowledge of vehicles who can help you assess any noticeable irregularities. We often forget small details when we leave situations and this is a sure way to go back and really see all the details.

I highly recommend sending a mechanic you know and trust to go to the location to do a thorough inspection. They usually charge around a hundred dollars to go to the vehicle and perform the inspection and less if you bring it to them. It will be money well spent either way. If the dealer or seller says no you cannot do an inspection, leave and don't waste your time. This is a more than obvious sign something is wrong.

Check out the blog post - How to check your fluids like a Girl @ www.girlsguidetocarbuying.com

Working in this business my entire life with certified mechanics and qualified sales people, I have learned to never accept someone's word for anything. I have witnessed all kinds of misrepresentations of vehicles and their condition from "qualified" people and I must say it is very disheartening. I believe a job should be done to the best of one's capabilities no matter what field you are in. That is why I emphasize learning the basics and putting in the effort to educate yourse

"Information Changes The Situation"

Trading Up

When trading in your vehicle you can minimize the amount you need to finance, IF you have equity in it. Do the homework on your current vehicle the same as you would with the one you are looking to purchase. Make sure to complete the **Current Vehicle Value Worksheet** before discussing a trade.

Another tip is to not inform the dealer that you are planning on a trade and shop as if you're going to purchase with no trade. It's best to get a price with no other complications, once you throw a trade in the mix the numbers work against you, leaving money on the table in their favor.

Work out your price first and get that number handled and then get yourself out of there. You can then return and decide to do a trade later. This way you have all the numbers in front of you and you are prepared. Be aware that dealers will pay wholesale prices for your trade and rightfully so, they have to prep it for retail, advertising costs, overhead, commissions and so on especially if they already have several of that make and model on the lot. I wouldn't get bent out of shape on this, I mean none of us would work for free. Just be reasonable and fair on your price but don't give it away.

If you decide to trade and the numbers make sense you will be able to apply the trade-in amount to your down payment. Also you will only pay sales tax on the difference. You can work out all the numbers in your **Purchase Planner Worksheet**. It might be a better deal for you to save on sales tax than trying to sell the vehicle on your own.

Always have your vehicle detailed and looking amazing, all your service records and a copy of your VHR (Vehicle History Report) when bringing it into the dealer to get a number on a trade as well as when you are showing it to a private buyer. This will ensure you get the most for the vehicle and also confirm the validity of your asking price. Leave no holes for a price reduction.

Current Vehicle WORKSHEET

Year_____   Make_____   Model_____

Miles_____   Color_____   MPG_____

Options_____

History Report_____   Service Records_____

Interior Cond._____   Exterior Cond._____

Tire Tread_____   Jack_____   Spare_____

Valid Inspection Sticker_____   Keys___   Owner's Manual_____

Trade-In Value_____   Cash Value_____

Payoff Amount_____   Monthly Payment_____ **OR** Title_____

Comps

Year_____   Year_____
Make_____   Make_____
Model_____   Model_____
Miles_____   Miles_____
Color_____   Color_____
History Report_____   History Report_____
Options_____   Options_____
Price_____   Price_____

Year_____   Year_____
Make_____   Make_____
Model_____   Model_____
Miles_____   Miles_____
Color_____   Color_____
History Report_____   History Report_____
Options_____   Options_____
Price_____   Price_____

Why Buy Used

The highest depreciation is on new vehicles, plummeting the minute you drive off the lot, turning it into a bonafide used vehicle and leaving the next girl to reap the benefits of a beautiful, less costly vehicle with a slower reduction in value. It is much easier to offset the depreciation on a used vehicle and retain some equity with a decent down payment.

Buying used is the best value for your money. The initial depreciation was absorbed and now you have a great vehicle that won't cost you a fortune as if you had purchased it new. Plus you can drive it for a few years, not worry about going over a mileage limit like in a lease and then sell it with some equity in it and go get another new used vehicle. This time upgrade because you successfully purchased the last one right.

If buying a certified pre-owned (CPO) vehicle makes you feel better about your purchase just make sure it is certified by the manufacturer or "factory." These CPO vehicles are only sold at a dealership that specializes in that franchise and who are authorized to do so. These vehicles are typically 5 years old or newer and less than 80,000 miles, so be sure CPO's you are interested in have these specifications. Expect to pay an average of a few thousand dollars more for a certified pre owned vehicle vs. a non certified one.

It really comes down to a personal decision and what feels right to you. Just always be sure to read the fine print and ask a lot of questions. Dealer-certified programs are often advertised as certified pre-owned but are only inspected within the dealership either by an employee or a hired third party, not by the manufacturer. They are usually sold with some type of extended service agreement or warranty.

 Feeling great about your decisions, finances and your purchase are what makes a great car buying experience. I definitely will say that used is the first step in finding yourself in a good place financially. You can get a vehicle with 1,000 miles or less that is considered used and has used values but is like brand spankin' new. The best bang for your buck! Just do the research, checklists and worksheets to get yourself the perfect vehicle for the right price and within budget.

In Business as
in Life, you don't get
what you deserve
you
get what you
negotiate

-Chester Karrass

Preparation

Good questions will discover everything. It's what you ask the sellers that will help confirm or deny the validity of the entire condition of the vehicle. The history, future and current value all play a part in the total package. Be thorough and ask everything you wish to know about the vehicle and always document the answers. This will save you time and narrow down the search as unsatisfactory answers will help eliminate vehicles that won't qualify for your standards of purchase.

Use the **Buyer's Questionnaire** to guide you during this process. These questions are good for both in person and phone interviews for dealers and private sellers. The more you know the better you will be able to assess certain criteria of the vehicle and perhaps take a closer look at a particular detail.

Buyer's Questionnaire

Vehicle History
some of these will not apply

Is it a 1 owner vehicle?

Are you the original owner?

Do you have the maintenance records on the vehicle?

Has anything recently been fixed or replaced on the vehicle?

How many keys do you have?

Is the owner's manual present?

Do you have the window sticker(buyers guide)?

Does it have a clean history report?

May I have the vin # ? _ _ _ _ _ _ _ _ _ _ _ _ _ _ _ _ _   (17 characters) unless older/classic

How many miles are on the vehicle?

Condition

Is it 4 wheel drive?
   Does it work properly?

Is it manual or automatic?

What options does it have?
(sunroof, navigation, power seats, bluetooth, leather, tire size, etc.)

Was it smoked in?

Were there pets that traveled in the vehicle?

Do all the windows and door locks work properly?

Is there any damage on the exterior or interior I should be aware of before I see the vehicle?

www.girlsguidetocarbuying.com   1-855-888-8522

How is the tire tread?

Are the brakes in good condition?

Does it have a valid inspection sticker?

Any chips or cracks in the windshield?

How is the paint?

Has it ever been re-painted or had body work?

Is there rust anywhere on the vehicle?

Does the A/C & Heater work properly?

Is there a spare tire and jack?

Does the vehicle have a factory / dealer or third party warranty?

Price

What's the asking price?

Is that based on the current market value?

Would you take cash?

Do you have the title?

Notes

A notice telling the buyer when the product that was just purchased will no longer function

—Richard Turner

Warranties

Research extended warranties before sitting down to purchase a vehicle. You can always purchase an extended warranty before the original manufacturer's warranty expires. It does not have to be obtained at the same time you get the vehicle. It can be something you think about and thoroughly go over before buying.

Extended warranties backed by the manufacturer are somewhat of an extension of the original warranty. However, there will be a deductible, per-repair deductible, repair location lock-ins and out of pocket pay outs. Be sure to go over all the terms of any warranty. There are different levels of warranties and they all have particular coverage specific to each tier.

> **TIP:** *When financing a vehicle warranties that are wrapped into the price will be part of your financing amount and you will be paying interest on that for the duration of your loan. Consider paying for warranties separately.*

You need to determine if it will be worth it for you to have the added cost of a warranty. Don't spend more on the extended warranty then you will on repairs during the length of time you will own the vehicle. It may be more sensible for you to set aside that money into a savings for maintenance and repairs if you have the discipline to reserve those savings.

BUYERS GUIDE

IMPORTANT: Spoken promises are difficult to enforce. Ask the dealer to put all promises in writing. Keep this form.

VEHICLE MAKE   MODEL   YEAR   VEHICLE IDENTIFICATION NUMBER (VIN)

WARRANTIES FOR THIS VEHICLE:

☐ **AS IS - NO DEALER WARRANTY**
THE DEALER DOES NOT PROVIDE A WARRANTY FOR ANY REPAIRS AFTER SALE.

☐ **DEALER WARRANTY**

☐ FULL WARRANTY.

☐ LIMITED WARRANTY. The dealer will pay ____% of the labor and ____% of the parts for the covered systems that fail during the warranty period. Ask the dealer for a copy of the warranty, and for any documents that explain warranty coverage, exclusions, and the dealer's repair obligations. *Implied warranties* under your state's laws may give you additional rights.

SYSTEMS COVERED: **DURATION:**

NON-DEALER WARRANTIES FOR THIS VEHICLE:

☐ MANUFACTURER'S WARRANTY STILL APPLIES. The manufacturer's original warranty has not expired on some components of the vehicle.

☐ MANUFACTURER'S USED VEHICLE WARRANTY APPLIES.

☐ OTHER USED VEHICLE WARRANTY APPLIES.

Ask the dealer for a copy of the warranty document and an explanation of warranty coverage, exclusions, and repair obligations.

☐ SERVICE CONTRACT. A service contract on this vehicle is available for an extra charge. Ask for details about coverage, deductible, price, and exclusions. If you buy a service contract within 90 days of your purchase of this vehicle, *implied warranties* under your state's laws may give you additional rights.

ASK THE DEALER IF YOUR MECHANIC CAN INSPECT THE VEHICLE ON OR OFF THE LOT.

OBTAIN A VEHICLE HISTORY REPORT AND CHECK FOR OPEN SAFETY RECALLS. For information on how to obtain a vehicle history report, visit ftc.gov/usedcars. To check for open safety recalls, visit safercar.gov. You will need the vehicle identification number (VIN) shown above to make the best use of the resources on these sites.

SEE OTHER SIDE for important additional information, including a list of major defects that may occur in used motor vehicles.

Si el concesionario gestiona la venta en español, pídale una copia de la Guía del Comprador en español.

BUYERS GUIDE

IMPORTANT: Spoken promises are difficult to enforce. Ask the dealer to put all promises in writing. Keep this form.

VEHICLE MAKE   MODEL   YEAR   VEHICLE IDENTIFICATION NUMBER (VIN)

WARRANTIES FOR THIS VEHICLE:

☐ IMPLIED WARRANTIES ONLY

The dealer doesn't make any promises to fix things that need repair when you buy the vehicle or afterward. But *implied warranties* under your state's laws may give you some rights to have the dealer take care of serious problems that were not apparent when you bought the vehicle.

☐ DEALER WARRANTY

☐ FULL WARRANTY.

☐ LIMITED WARRANTY. The dealer will pay ____% of the labor and ____% of the parts for the covered systems that fail during the warranty period. Ask the dealer for a copy of the warranty, and for any documents that explain warranty coverage, exclusions, and the dealer's repair obligations. *Implied warranties* under your state's laws may give you additional rights.

SYSTEMS COVERED: **DURATION:**

NON-DEALER WARRANTIES FOR THIS VEHICLE:

☐ MANUFACTURER'S WARRANTY STILL APPLIES. The manufacturer's original warranty has not expired on some components of the vehicle.

☐ MANUFACTURER'S USED VEHICLE WARRANTY APPLIES.

☐ OTHER USED VEHICLE WARRANTY APPLIES.

Ask the dealer for a copy of the warranty document and an explanation of warranty coverage, exclusions, and repair obligations.

☐ SERVICE CONTRACT. A service contract on this vehicle is available for an extra charge. Ask for details about coverage, deductible, price, and exclusions. If you buy a service contract within 90 days of your purchase of this vehicle, *implied warranties* under your state's laws may give you additional rights.

ASK THE DEALER IF YOUR MECHANIC CAN INSPECT THE VEHICLE ON OR OFF THE LOT.

OBTAIN A VEHICLE HISTORY REPORT AND CHECK FOR OPEN SAFETY RECALLS. For information on how to obtain a vehicle history report, visit ftc.gov/usedcars. To check for open safety recalls, visit safercar.gov. You will need the vehicle identification number (VIN) shown above to make the best use of the resources on these sites.

SEE OTHER SIDE for important additional information, including a list of major defects that may occur in used motor vehicles.

Si el concesionario gestiona la venta en español, pídale una copia de la Guía del Comprador en español.

Here is a list of some major defects that may occur in used vehicles.

Frame & Body
Frame-cracks, corrective welds, or rusted through
Dog tracks—bent or twisted frame

Engine
Oil leakage, excluding normal seepage
Cracked block or head
Belts missing or inoperable
Knocks or misses related to camshaft lifters and push rods
Abnormal exhaust discharge

Transmission & Drive Shaft
Improper fluid level or leakage, excluding normal seepage
Cracked or damaged case which is visible
Abnormal noise or vibration caused by faulty transmission or drive shaft
Improper shifting or functioning in any gear
Manual clutch slips or chatters

Differential
Improper fluid level or leakeage, excluding normal seepage
Cracked of damaged housing which is visible
Abnormal noise or vibration caused by faulty differential

Cooling System
Leakage including radiator
Improperly functioning water pump

Electrical System
Battery leakage
Improperly functioning alternator, generator, battery, or starter

Fuel System
Visible leakage

Inoperable Accessories
Gauges or warning devices
Air conditioner
Heater & Defroster

Brake System
Failure warning light broken
Pedal not firm under pressure (DOT spec.)
Not enough pedal reserve (DOT spec.)
Does not stop vehicle in straight line (DOT spec.)
Hoses damaged
Drum or rotor too thin (Mfgr. Specs)
Lining or pad thickness less than 1/32 inch
Power unit not operating or leaking
Structural or mechanical parts damaged

Air Bags

Steering System
Too much free play at steering wheel (DOT specs.)
Free play in linkage more than 1/4 inch
Steering gear binds or jams
Front wheels aligned improperly (DOT specs.)
Power unit belts cracked or slipping
Power unit fluid level improper

Suspension System
Ball joint seals damaged
Structural parts bent or damaged
Stabilizer bar disconnected
Spring broken
Shock absorber mounting loose
Rubber bushings damaged or missing
Radius rod damaged or missing
Shock absorber leaking or functioning improperly

Tires
Tread depth less than 2/32 inch
Sizes mismatched
Visible damage

Wheels
Visible cracks, damage or repairs
Mounting bolts loose or missing

Exhaust System
Leakage
Catalytic Converter

DEALER NAME

ADDRESS

TELEPHONE   EMAIL

FOR COMPLAINTS AFTER SALE, CONTACT:

IMPORTANT: The information on this form is part of any contract to buy this vehicle. Removing this label before consumer purchase (except for purpose of test-driving) violates federal law (16 C.F.R. 455).

Do Not Bite At The Bait Of Pleasure, Til You Know There Is No Hook Beneath It

- Thomas Jefferson

Hook Line Sinker

Beware too good to be true ads--they are. Almost every ad I come across are sleazy ways to get you into the dealership on false promises. Similar to going out and having someone tell you anything to get you home. This is the sole purpose of bait ads. To trick you into thinking it's a great deal just to be lured into a web of lies and deceit.

The FTC requires that dealers' ads must state clearly the terms of the offer and discounts and how you may qualify for them. Despite this law, dealers may not disclose this information properly or at all. You may not get the truth until you're in the F&I office, halfway through a deal.

Be very cautious and leery of any ad and always read the fine print, call and ask questions and protect yourself. They most likely just want to get you there and then sell you on other vehicles, products and services. Most of the time the qualifications for those ads are extremely narrow and only pertain to a very very small group of individuals, if at all.

Expect The Yes. Embrace The No. That's How You Master The Close!

Closing The Deal

If you have asked, answered, and computed all the defense methods in this book, first I want to say I am extremely proud of you! It is a lot of work but totally worth it. You now have the knowledge and capability to go proudly negotiate the purchase of your vehicle independently confident without any doubt. In the end it truly comes down to you. It may seem a little scary or uncomfortable but these are feelings of growth and success so never shy away from them. March yourself straight on the path to that vehicle you have chosen and get it on your terms at your price that you know is undeniably accurate and fair.

You have done your homework, made a decision, put everything into place-- now go make the commitment. Go freaking negotiate a deal and get what you want! Don't ever be afraid to go after the the things you want and deserve. Sometimes even when we don't get those things we learn invaluable lessons about ourselves. Reap the benefits of your hard work and go enjoy the ride!

Congratulations!

She Who Dares Wins

girlsguidetocarbuying.com

Resources

Car Value Websites
titlekeycash.com
kbb.com
edmunds.com
truecar.com
carsense.com
carmax.com
iSeeCars.com
EbayMotors.com
NADAguides.com

Vehicle History Reports
autocheck.com
CarFax.com
vehiclehistory.gov
ftc.gov/usedcars

Vehicle Research
Autoblog
Craigslist
Facebook Groups
allpar.com
safecar.gov

Motor Vehicle
NMVTIS
dmv.org
aamva.org

Insurance
NICB.org
iii.org

Lending
asmarterchoice.org
CUNA.org
consumer.ftc.gov

www.ingramcontent.com/pod-product-compliance
Lightning Source LLC
Chambersburg PA
CBHW061403090426
42743CB00003B/123